Listening for Sirens

P J Kimber

Listening for Sirens

Copyright © P J Kimber 2011

ISBN 978-1-4709-0037-3

P J Kimber has asserted her right under Section 77 of the Copyright, Designs and Patents Act 1988 to be identified as the author of this work.

All rights reserved. No part of this book may be reproduced, stored in a retrieval system, or transmitted in any form, or by any means, electronic, mechanical, photocopying, recording or otherwise without prior written permission from the Copyright owner.

Published by *PK Publications*
Printed by Lulu.com

Cover photo: *Buddha Reflections* by P J Kimber

Contact: penny@riversidewriters.co.uk

To my mother
Alison Brown

Acknowledgements

Grateful thanks are due to the editors of the following publications in which some of these poems first appeared: *A Werry Whaplode* (The Riverside Writers); *Book of Dreams, A Poem For Christmas, National Poetry Anthology 2011* (United Press).

Thanks to *The Riverside Writers* for their support, encouragement and help with editing, especially to Karen Hopley for advice on layout; to the *Gallery* at Warrington's Bank Quay House for hosting our meetings, and to *Warrington Poetry Group* where many of these poems were first performed.

Contents

9	Anniversary
10	Night Terrors
11	Medusa
13	Anna
14	Pothole
16	Dropping
17	Rebel
18	Sharing
19	Another Place
21	Herem
23	Moving House
24	Christmas Eve
25	Doll's House
26	Answers
27	Snog Off
28	Empty Nest
29	Callie's Class
30	Free Lunch
31	Sleep Safely
32	Journey
34	Playground
35	A-Z Paranoia
36	Bedding Plantoum
37	A Sign of the Times
39	Stalemate
40	Paper Day

41	Bird Watching
42	Ticket
43	Kettering Revisited
46	Summer '76
47	Prescription
48	Nugget
49	Secret weapon
51	Paper City
52	Donation
53	Bus Stop
55	Anticipating *The Deathly Hallows*
57	Eating Cheese at Midnight
58	Mr Universe
59	It's Snowing
61	Listening for Sirens
62	Perfect Wedding
65	Quick Brown Fox
66	The Icing on the Cake
67	For Geoffrey
68	Floreat Verbum
69	Intensive Care
71	For Barbara
72	The Smell of Wet Cats
73	Mothering Sunday
75	Forgotten
76	Rachel
78	Slide Viewer
79	Alone

Anniversary

The third Scotch-on-the-rocks loosens his tie,
the fourth his inhibitions and his tongue.
Another, and he'll either cry, or try
to make a pass at me. Although I'm young
I recognize the signs: the addled joke
of stale fidelity, the pale excuse
of boredom, lost excitement. Here's a bloke
who wears domestic duty as a noose.
His present stands between us like the ghost
of marriage past, unwrapped, unworn – cashmere.
The woollen anniversary. "A toast!"
he winks, raising his glass, "Another year!"
There's a suggestion – faint, yet I catch it –
a seven year itch. But, should I scratch it?

Night Terrors

I'm frantic. I've been calling for an hour
And seven minutes. I have clinked the dish.
A call, a clink has no coercive power.

I scour the garden, prey to their wild whim;
I scrape the foil from daylight-saving dusk
For jackpot images: a pair of paws. *Ker-ching!*

I'm thinking dogs: rat-catching terriers;
I'm thinking greyhounds closing on a hare;
I'm thinking foxes: stinking snap-neck jaws.

I'm thinking Curiosity: shed doors
Slammed shut by wind or human hand –
Starvation is a slow and lonely end.

I'm thinking poachers, nooses, gin-traps, snares;
I'm thinking kidnap, catnap, pelts and skin.
I'm thinking fur coats, Cruella de Vil.

I'm thinking posters: *Missing! Burmese cats.*
I'm thinking of a £1000 Reward.
I'm thinking trees: faint, stranded miaows unheard.

I'm thinking barbed wire fence – a misjudged jump –
Pale clumps of blood-stained fur snagged on the wire.
I'm thinking of the road and cars…

Hours later when they saunter home unharmed
And unrepentant, dew damp from the night,
I'm so pleased I could hug them both to death.

Medusa

Every day's a bad hair day!
And now I think I'm going *grey*.
Give me a break, for pity's sake –
it's tricky with a head of snakes:
a writhing, knotted reptile mane
rules out most styles.
And when they slough their skin – believe you me –
the dandruff joke is wearing pretty thin.
I'm not complaining, but
even when I nicely ask for something plain and simple
like a cut and blow,
the answer's a resounding, 'No!'

I'd settle for a trim,
but still the stylist's looking grim
as though my scalp's a seething nest of lice.
My chances of a razor cut are slim.
"It's more than s-snipping off a few s-split ends,"
he stammers, staring at my squirming friends.
At least he has the manners to reply;
most hairdressers won't look me in the eye.
They stand in stony silence, or they mumble an excuse:
"Shampoo? It's no can do.
 We're booked up solid, Miss Medusa."

Today my luck has changed. The new guy's name
is Perseus, and he's a real charmer. I'll admit
the lad is *fit*. No hang ups either about fangs
or venom; didn't blink an eyelid
at the flickering forked tongues,
and giggled when the python crushed the brush and
                                        swallowed it.
 O to be young and innocent again!

You'd think back-combing serpent-headed Gorgons was a
game.
"So, how about a perm?" I asked.
"What? With those wriggling worms?" he laughed.
"Highlights?"
"Not if they bite. I'd never get the foils
around the coils. Medusa, if I may,
I'd like to try a radical new look today."

The snakes hissed but he fed them baby mice
until, replete, they fell asleep, all basking
in the heat under the drier.
Our eyes met in the mirror. He didn't flinch.
"Another inch or two ...
A clean cut and it's in the bag," he said.
I thought he meant my hair and not my head.

Anna

Anna, your Siamese king I'll be.
Without a governess, a queen
To school my lawless monarchy, it's
Anarchy…

Anna, transcending time and place,
You're Nefertiti's iPod, Cleopatra's phone,
You're Helen's thousand rocket ships in space.
Anachronism.

Anna, my Amazonian fantasy,
Bare-breasted, tall, magnificent,
(Ideally stripped and up against a wall.)
Anaglypta.

Anna, my slinky temptress,
Must I guess what coiled charms kink
Beneath your rippling, peristaltic curves?
Anaconda.

Anna, my palindromic paramour,
My protean, top-scoring Scrabble-child,
My versatile enigma.
Anagram.

Anna, what vase, what vessel can enclose
The love that overflows the grail?
I've poured my heart into your jar –
An amphora.

Anna, I'm proud to shout your name
Out loudly and with emphasis
Again and – for the heck of it – again.
Anaphora.

Pothole

I am here, waiting.
You don't see me at first,
then I catch your eye
- the jolt of recognition -
and, boy, you positively swerve
to avoid me. You just can't get away
fast enough. Never mind. You'll be back.
I'll be here, waiting.

I'm still here, waiting
for you. Where are you going?
There are things we need
to say. I'm growing by the day …
I used to be so flat and firm.
Is that what makes you turn away?

Maybe I'll catch you unawares.
Don't be scared.
Don't you trust me any more?
I'm hungry for you.
I could eat you up;
I could swallow you whole.

I used to be so grounded,
level-headed, so together.
Where did it get me? Waiting
on the road to nowhere.
No more. I plan to make it big.
You'll say I'm flaky, that I've cracked,
I've caved, I'm raving, but you'll see.
You'll read my name in lights
- red, amber, green.
I tell you, I'll be breath-taking;
I'll turn heads.
I'll stop traffic.

In your eyes, I don't measure up.
Don't be so quick to judge.
I'm not as shallow as you think.
I've talent, hidden depths.
Don't be shy; come over here
and take the plunge. I'm waiting.
Let's bump and grind.

I'll rock your world.
I'll burst your tyre.
I'll snap your axle.

Dropping

Dropping ...　like a penny in a Wishing Well,
　　　　　　like a clanger from a broken bell,

　　　　　　like a dew-drip from a sniffy nose,
　　　　　　like flies, like famous names, like hammer blows ...

　　　　　　like the mercury before a shower,
　　　　　　like the petals of a wilted flower,

　　　　　　like a conker from a chestnut tree,
　　　　　　like my stomach when you smile at me,

　　　　　　like a stitch in time, too late to save the rest,
　　　　　　like the sunset sinking in the west,

　　　　　　like a pin into a silent hall,
Dropping ...　like your faces as you watch me fall.

Rebel

My hemline sits demurely on the knee;
flat, regulation shoes - black lace-up brogues;
a uniform school blouse, top-buttoned, tucked
behind the neatly knotted 6th Form tie.

Long hair tied back; unvarnished nails cut short;
I don't sport tats or piercings; all my bling,
bold jewellery is left at home, unworn.
My tights are tawny beige or natural fawn.

I never answer back or cheek the staff;
don't chat in lessons, text or Tweet or chew.
I sit right at the front; I walk, don't run.
My library books are never overdue.

My homework's always handed in on time;
I don't skip class to catch the early bus
nor nip behind the bike sheds for a fag –
they won't find booze or ciggies in my bag.

I'm *Goody-Two-Shoes*; butter wouldn't melt.
I count the cards and play the hand I'm dealt,
anonymous, like trained professional spies.
A bland low profile is the best disguise.

If I am *Teachers' Pet*, they're blinkered fools.
In loving you I'm breaking <u>all</u> the rules.

Sharing

At some point in the night
you slip in between the sheets
without waking me,
heat-seeking, sunflower faced,
encroaching, wine-spill-spreading,
dough-expanding, subtle hijacking
of warmth and space.
You mould your limber length
along the contours of my back,
unfolding, poaching,
inching closer, pushing
till I'm cold and clinging to the mattress edge,
a climber bivouacking on a ledge.
Awake, I claw my rightful way back in.
I feel your four paws press against my skin.

Another Place *Crosby Beach, 2006*

Ahoy!
We are the iron men, the iron men, the iron men –
Deployed with military precision,
Stranded in a no man's land of sand,
We're cast ashore like ship-wrecked sentinels.
We stand to attention; we scan the horizon.

Hi!
We are the iron men, the iron men, the iron men –
The Gormley guys: his height, his size.
If you and he were introduced you'd think
You'd met somewhere before.
I didn't recognise you with your clothes on,
You might say.

Hey!
We are the iron men, the iron men, the iron men –
We're cloned in his own image.
Bare-bummed arrogance!
A race of faceless Antonies –
Production-line metallic blasphemy.

Oi!
We are the iron men, the iron men, the iron men –
The butts of cheeky ridicule:
"Let's hoist his Jolly Roger," mock
the sneering, barrel-bellied trippers,
shorts and seaside flip-flops flapping.
Wrapping scarves they dress and strip us,
Cheering yappy mutts that cock and piddle,
Leering, jeering, happy-slapping.

Ohh...
We are the iron men, the iron men, the iron men –
As powerless as nude Canutes.
Salute while rising waves
Devour our brothers, starting with their feet
Like Jelly Babies.
Every tide another genocide.

Ow!
We are the iron men, the iron men, the iron men –
The salt stings in our wounds.
Exposure brings corrosion, tarnish, rust.
It is the way of things. We're Zen.
We're reconciled to our mortality
And borrowing the beaches while we can.

Tomorrow's sails are filling, free, unfurled:
We look west, watching for a brave New World.

He-rem

With a nod to Billy Joel

What's the problem with the male population?
Have the real men all disappeared?
Don't apply unless you're slim, fit and solvent,
And, ideally, without a beard.
Wrap your tongue around some romantic patter;
Old guys, young guys, size doesn't matter.
Don't snore? Don't smoke? Call yourself a new bloke?
Then sign on for my He-rem.

See him kitted out in skin tight leathers
And a helmet straight from outer space.
See the speedo creeping up past a hundred …
I start praying for the human race.
Took me riding on his chrome cruiser Harley,
Tripping faster than a quick sniff of Charlie.
Rev-head, Judge Dred, tiger tat for street cred.
A biker boy in my He-rem.

I've been courted by a hot-shot lawyer
But he turned my life into a trial –
Cross-examined for the least misdemeanour.
Truth or Justice? I lived in denial.
Say *pro bono*, but claim your expenses;
Your case is only as good as your defence is.
Slider, libel, swear it on the bible.
A Q.C. in my He-rem.

This one's chat up line is cross-pollination,
Germination, tons per acre yield,
Livestock, arable and cropping rotation.
Herd the cows into the bottom field,
Load the trailer, take the lambs to the market.
I'll drive the tractor; don't expect me to park it.
Combines, bale-twines, make hay while the sun shines.
A farmer in my He-rem.

What's the matter, don't you like it in purdah?
Wear your burkah; fasten your yashmak.
Folks would think that I was asking for murder.
Stay behind the screen; don't answer back.
For I have it on the best information,
The perfect man exists – in my imagination.
Dream on, scheme on, slap the whipping cream on,
And sign on for my He-rem.

Moving House

Removal men in bulging overalls
Ripped through the jilted building like a tide,
Swept out a lifetime's silt
And left a wake of boxes stacked head high -
Packed, crated chaos - jetsam on the drive.

Each of my eggshell, eye-bright seven years
Is tissue wrapped.
And whales the size of caravans
Have swallowed up my home.

If twenty minutes seemed an age
To scuff my uncollected thoughts
Outside the gates
And wave my classmates "Bye"
As one by one they ebbed away on foot,
Or flowed into the arms of punctual school-run mums,
Then forty were enough to snuff out hope.

Since breakfast I'd become
A waif, a foundling cuckoo child
Without a nest.
No known address. Adrift.
I waited for the lift that never came.

Christmas Eve

The keyhole brimmed with secrets. Whispers thrilled
the furtive dark. Beneath the advent door
a chink of spilled light drew me like a star.
The stillness teemed with hope.
Anticipation winked. I pressed
whorled ear prints in the wood grain, heard the rasp
of saw blades; tap, tip-tap, a hammer;
whirr-chug-whirr, the sprint of stitching;
scissors snip-snip-snip…

Silence. A pins and needle pause.
Footsteps…
Heart stops.
A guilty, gasped free diver's breath:
a barefoot spy, pyjama-poised for flight,
sloe-tongued, unripe excuses clamouring
for air.

Tap… Whirr… The murmured workshop noise resumed
as though the elves had come back to the room.
No wiser now but reassured, I slunk
upstairs to hang my stocking on my bunk.

Doll's House

The walls are all the games he never played;
The staircase, spiral secrets left unshared;
The rooms, exciting plans he never made;
The windows are the soul he never bared;
The gables are the cuddles left unhugged,
The attic, bedtime stories still unread;
The wiring is his heartstring, slack, untugged;
The lights, soft words of comfort never said;
The doors, the praise he seldom dreamed to voice;
The chimney, bridges burned and not rebuilt;
The floor, harsh rules that left no room for choice;
The gleaming paintwork glosses over guilt.
Displays of love were frowned upon, taboo.
He built a doll's house. That would have to do.

Answers

Who?
Who do you think? Who's who at the zoo.
Why?
Why indeed!
That's for me to know and you to find out.
What?
Don't say what, say pardon.
When?
When the time comes.
Where?
There and back again.
How?
How!
How long?
…is a piece of string?
How many?
…beans make five?
How much?
Money and fair words.
How old?
As old as my tongue and a little bit older than my teeth.

After a while,
You just stop asking.

Snog Off !

No kissing on Warrington station;
No pashing and no sucking face.
Prolonged lippy-suction
Causes an obstruction,
And Bank Quay does not have the space.

The timetable tyrants have spoken:
No cuddling – schedules can't wait.
The council by-laws
Say, *Stand clear of the doors*,
The platform's no place for a date.

No smooching at Warrington Central.
Canoodling has also been banned.
Indulging your ardour
Makes parting much harder
- Make do with a shake of the hand.

No public displays of affection;
No lingering, loving farewells.
Exceed your kiss quota
By one puckering iota
And you'll set off the sirens and bells.

The sign read: *French Kissing Forbidden*
Till somebody said it was racist.
We're now not allowed
To embrace in a crowd.
Excuse me, but isn't that spacist?

So why do the trains run so slowly?
Are they stranded in snow, stuck in fog?
Do leaves on the line
Stop them running on time,
Or is it the wrong sort of snog?

Empty Nest

I can't say I've been feathering my nest.
With this loud, hungry brood there's nowt to spare.
But when they're fledged and gone,
there'll be more room to move.
I'll spread my wings.

Callie's Class
For C M

All hail! I raise my arms to greet
the sun; a seismic rift
propels me forward. Glide-winged, mute,
I swan dive, fold. *Exhale.*
Shape-shifter: I am stiff, a Plank;
a squirming Caterpillar – *hold* –
a Stick Insect uncurls a Cobra's hood;
flex, bend – *inhale* – to Upward Dog (good boy!);
extend to Downward Dog, Inverted V.
Inhale, exhale. OK. When can I *breathe*?
Yo, Sun! G'day, hello, how do you do?

A Cat, a Hare, a Locust, Fish, a Crow,
an Eagle, Pigeon, Dolphin, Crocodile,
a Tortoise, Cow-faced Lion … (I'm versatile.)
Somehow the world is standing on its head
while I'm an aviary, a petting zoo.
A Lotus flower, a Tree, a Plough, a Staff,
a Bridge, a Bow, a Gate, a Lightning Bolt,
a Table, Chair, a Triangle, a Boat.
Just watch me morph.
My limbs are Plasticine.

An Archer, Cobbler, Dancer … I'm a Jill
of all trades, multi-tasking: balance, stretch,
twist, focus, still the mind; relax and smile.
A fighting force of leg-splayed Warriors kneel,
surrender, finding peace: Pose of a Child.

I'm panting mantras when I should be chanting:
Shanti, shanti,
Om, Om, Om. Namaste.

Free Lunch

Thanks for the invitation. I'd as soon
strip naked and evacuate my bowels
in public as dine out.

The menu lists hot ashes, sawdust, straw,
iron filings, granite chips, soil, gravel, grit.
The tasteful paper has as much appeal.

For starters, pan fried pebbles with crushed bone?
Or throw all caution to the winds, plump
for paupiettes of freshly quarried stone.

The entrée next: I'll choose the hammer-toe-nail salad
and a side of shredded navel fluff
served on a bed of sun-dried sand.

Dessert? I'll pass. Slate-layered mille-feuilles,
snow-capped dandruff meringue,
will crumble to chalk powder on my tongue.

Some wine? A bottle of your best house spit
will fit the bill, though I shall stick to water
while I sit here savouring my hunger.

The waiter is waiting to take my disorder.

Sleep Safely

Gustav Klimt, 'Baby Cradle'

No pastel pink for my sleeping princess.
I'll swaddle you in braided bands of gold
With swathes of coral, scarlet, verdigris,
Jade green and azure blue, vermillion swirls
And turquoise curlicues for my best girl.

There's wool for warmth; fresh cotton's crisp and cool;
Light lawn and muslin soft upon your skin.
Let me unspool your calico cocoon;
Unfurl the boutique butterfly within.

I'll bundle you in bolts of rolled brocade
And vibrant, brash, bazaar-bright sari silk,
A jacquard jungle, paisley, floral chintz
And boldly clashing geometric prints.

A bedrock layer of linen, interlocked
With veins of royal velvet, brocatelle,
Chenille, organza, poplin, crepe de chine,
With tiers of taffeta; a satin seam:
A blanket mantle fitting for a queen.

Sleep safely, muffled baby, while I pile
Your cradle high with quilted blessings, strew
A tapestry of textile tenderness.
I'll cushion you from care, my cherub child,
- out there the world's uncovered, cold and wild -
Enfold you in the fabric of my love.

Journey

My father packs and then repacks the boot,
precision drilled, as though the cases had to meet and
intersect half-way,
touch noses, greet each other; bursting luggage moles,
their tunnels boring through Mount Holiday.

Co-pilot, mother, counting down for take-off, ticks her list.
One.　　Fridge defrosted. Check.
Two.　　Milk and papers cancelled. Check.
Three.　Cat food in the kitchen; key with neighbour. Check.
Four.　　Electrical appliances unplugged. Check.
　　　　(And double-check. You can't take any chances.)
Five.　　Back door bolted. Windows shut. Check. Check.
　　　　Tick. Tick.

Shoe-horned into the back seat, chafing, pent;
new jelly sandals rubbing sore pink weals
across our heels before we've even left the drive.
Divided by a pile of scratchy towels,
snorkels and flippers, hats, the 'changing-tent'
stuffed in a canvas hold-all which,
for no apparent reason, mother calls the Berlin Wall.

Inside the hot, corked car the air ferments
the scent of holidays: salt, seaside, sand;
the surf boards' newly varnished resin tang
(my brother catches waves,
while I catch only scoops of gravel in my bathing suit,
and graze my toes);
the underlying whiff of fish - of reels, nets, rods,
dried maggots, possibly, or rotting worms.

Like mothballs in a party mood
our bags exude a skunky suntan lotion niff,

the oily, citrus, sour-sweat, soap-defying smell
of shoulder-burning, blister-popping days,
of red-raw, chalky Calamine-daubed nights
in tin drum caravans with whispering, gas-mantle lights.

This summer, proudly, I spell out the dashboard list:
Bicester to Chipping Norton, Tewkesbury
to Hereford, then Ross and Hay-on-Wye.
Just names. I'll navigate my way:
the lay-by where we stop to buy fresh plums;
the side road where we picnic in the rain;
grass verges where we compete to be sick.

We've played out *Spot the Post Box* and it's time now for *I Spy*.
My brother starts. " – with my little eye,
something beginning with S."
I guess at shoes and socks and shorts and spade and suntan cream.
"It's Spider!" he exclaims. I scream. He laughs. I cry.

I wake and can no longer read the signs.
The names are full of Ll's and Ww's and Dd's;
they sound like gargled gulps of gob and spit.
My brother tweaks my hair and hisses, "Psst!
D'you know the Welsh word for 'hello' is 'Shit'?"

Now, like the chorus of an old, familiar song,
my mother thinks she's left the oven on;
my father growls, "The rear suspension's shot."
My brother's hungry, thirsty, bored, squashed, sticky, hot...
"Are we there yet?"
"Who's first to see the sea?"
Let it be me. Oh, please, let it be me.

Playground

Bigger boys, too tall for the turnstile,
Scale the stockade,
Invade the corral,
Stolen ball
Teasing between them.
In the middle we're all piggies,
Squealing.

Bigger boys, whipping the roundabout …
Giving it top spin.
Reeling toddlers shoot
From the spokes
Like sparks
From a Catherine Wheel.

Bigger boys, bombing the see-saw.
Playground trebuchet:
Cannonball kids.

Bigger boys, storming the slide:
Full-frontal assault,
Taking it at a run.
Jolting descent. Sticking.
Older and wider.

A-Z Paranoia

Don't quote me ... I suspect the small black spots
Denoting stations, London's underground
Tube network, are encrypted *microdots*
Containing information which, if found
And analysed, might grossly compromise
Our national security. The code
Has taken years to crack. *(I fear the spies
Who lurk on corners with the bears ...)* Each road
Or street conceals a secret cryptograph;
The very names are ciphers. No one knows
What messages the dots disguise - don't laugh -
What plots. Look at the scope. I shall expose
Conspiracy, clandestine rendezvous:
"9.45, B6, page 52."

Bedding Plantoum

Just plant the £10 notes and watch them rot,
instead of buying bedding plants in spring.
We might as well stick fivers in a pot
of compost. They won't come to anything.

Instead of buying bedding plants, in spring
- sometimes - we sow a packetful of seeds
in compost. They won't come to anything;
our seedlings die or mutate into weeds.

Sometimes we sow a packetful of seeds
which always fail to thrive. Or, if they sprout,
our seedlings die or mutate into weeds
in May. We buy some ready to prick out,

which also fail to thrive; or, if they sprout,
they make a juicy feast for greedy bugs.
In May we buy some ready to prick out –
we're growing bedding plants to feed the slugs.

They make a juicy feast for greedy bugs –
we might as well stick fivers in a pot.
We're growing bedding plants to feed the slugs –
just plant the £10 notes and watch them rot.

A Sign of the Times

Stuff me in wet Wellingtons;
wrap me round your chips;
treat me like a doormat;
tear me into strips;
lay me in the litter tray
beneath an inch of grit;
let me line your bottom drawer
- cut me till I fit.

Tuck me round a homeless chest
to ward off winter chills;
roll me up and twist me
into fire-lighting spills;
crush me in an oblong mould
that shapes me into bricks;
burn me up instead of coal
or coke or logs or sticks.

Rip me into pieces;
smother me in PVA;
build me up in sticky layers
of *papier maché*;
practise origami with
a pleat, a tuck, a nip;
fold me up into a swan,
a rose, a hat, a ship.

Mulch me round your bedding plants
to choke out weeds and bugs;
press me into flower pots –
make eco-friendly plugs;
keep me damp and sprout a crop
of mustard, cress and greens;
spread me on the table top
in case you spill the beans.

Take a wad and wipe me
on your windows till they shine.
pack me round your valuables,
your ornaments and china.
raise me like a barrier
of words to hide behind;
place me in a capsule
for posterity to find.

Buy me for my crosswords,
games and quizzes, Sudokus,
but God forbid you'd ever choose
to *read* me for the news.

Stalemate

We have burned the candle-ends of indifference,
Moulding civility from warm wax;
Icarus smiles.
The flame gutters.
Smoke screens the gulf
Between our silences,
Melting familiarity
Pinned like a wanton voodoo doll
Breeding contempt.
It will be a long night.
At the top of the stairs
Our lives taper
Into separate rooms.

Paper Day

I'm going to fold my day into a plane
And throw it at the sky.
I'll crane to track its arrow-head trajectory,
The rising sweep of its unswerving arc.
I'll watch it spear the future on a spike
Like orders in a busy restaurant;
Stream kite-tail sharp tomorrows in its slip.
Proposal banners trail, trite slogans flap.
I'll watch it lose momentum, stall;
Its sycamore, slow-waltzing fall,
Crash-landing with a bloodied, Concorde nose.

I'm going to crush my day into a ball
And toss it at the bin,
Or chuck it for the puppy-dog to chase.
He drops it, chewed and slimy, at my feet;
He wags and grins. I juggle it from hand to hand.
A feint... a pass... a scrimmage on the floor.
If I regain possession I can choose
To flatten out its creases, smooth
Away the wasted hours and play again
Or scrunch it up like yesterday's old news.

I'm going to twist my day into a spill
And light it at one end
To set the tinder world ablaze –
Blue papers torching at its firebrand touch.
I'll brandish it until my fingers scorch,
Until the taper page burns grey,
A curling, worm cast whorl of fallen ash
Amidst the reams of time.

Bird Watching

The promise of a secret plover's nest ...
Her trusting, tiny fist gloved in his palm,
They pick their way, walking in silence, lest
They scare the peeping chicks. He pulls her arm
And tips her down amidst tall grass to spy,
Unseen, a calming finger on her lip.
No talk: the birds will take alarm and fly.
His other hand is working on his zip.
She can identify a snipe, a tern,
A curlew by its cry. He's taught her names
For all the common gulls, and, in return,
She learned the rules of special big boy games.
No fear, no blame; she's shamelessly complicit,
And bares her private place and dares him kiss it.

Ticket

Barely more than subliminal
I sensed the shot,
And sideways, in the corner of my eye,
I spied the flash
That killed my innocence,
That made me criminal.

No, "Smile please; say cheese!"
No time to primp or tease my limp hair into a style;
No time to pose or pout or do a Princess Di –
Peep coyly out from under lowered lids.
Too late I bit the brakes.
The candid lens had focused on my fate,
My number plate.
No warning. Just my luck.
It sucked. The camera clicked
And wrecked my morning. Nicked.

Kettering Revisited

Nit-picking a parental path
past church-yard to the market place,
mined with a host of memories
now buried with the teenage ghosts,
reminders of a life sloughed for this body-guardian role,
armed with coiled nonchalance, I stroll.

'Enough's enough. Boys, don't be rough.'
Brace for a Jedi ambush (feign surprise).
Invoke the Force. Will Luke prevail?
Darth Vader's head falls at a sabre stroke.
The Rebels rout the Empire. Space
reverberates with boyish glee
(a plaster for Skywalker's knee).
    Heroic imagination
    of a second generation.
    (My Han was never digitally remastered.)

These Friday stalls are skeletal,
bare trestle squares, like undressed hoops
reduced from swathes of skirt and drape
to wooden-slatted underwear.

On bustling, hustling Market Day,
leaving my harassed mum to cope
with coins and change, more veg than she had arms,
I'd slope away
and sidle through the fruits and flapping fabrics
to the books;
idling, peruse the tatty ranks
of second-hand best sellers, hoping for
Dick Francis or an Alistair MacClean,
or, later, Gibran, Hesse or R.D. Laing.

She always knew just where to look.
With bulging bags, white-fingered, Mum
reclaimed me for the mud-caked greens
and, bullet-proof with spuds and beans,
laid tracks through lesser shoppers like a tank.

The High Street, my old spending ground,
extends a manicured and Arndale hand
in civil greeting, polished, tinted,
with no hint of recognition.
Tastefully accessorised,
block-paved and pedestrianized,
the proffered cheek retail suburban chic,
more C&A than Jaeger.
As an outsider now I meet
this former friend
who's 'had her colours done' just for a treat.

Bargain hunters! New Year browsers!
Sale time vultures, scavengers
who rend the entrails, scour last season's stock
of tops, socks, stockings, blouses, trousers.
Apologetic present swappers
clutching creased excuses, bills, receipts;
word perfect in Consumer Rights
and spoiling for their annual fight
with Christmas-cursing Tracey at the till.

Adrift on the spending sea
- we're treading time until the matinee –
I count the bobbing boys repeatedly
and watch the waves for synchronicity.

Stop! Waterstones! A haven from the tide.
We plunge inside, drop anchor, fleeces, gloves
to bask within its literary lagoon.

Boys moored, dipping in the shallows
(Goosebumps, Dahl and Dick-King-Smith),
methodically I comb the shelving shores
- OK, call me a Booker backlog bore -
checking the subject sections, just in case ...
half-hoping, at each aisle, to see your face.

And later, when I calculate the odds
of meeting, after all these years and miles,
'infinitesimal' is my best guess.
The gods were very kind.

... Watching you pay and then walk away;
Willing your eyes to find mine
and acknowledge my stare;
daring you to be real.

Scanning your lines for a sign of denial,
poised to retreat with a breezy adieu;
distilling two decades to drops in phial;
honing my life to a hurried haiku.

Squeezing your hand for too long and then longer;
and becoming eighteen in your smile.

Summer '76

The year the algae bloomed,
the duck-weed ran amuck, mushroomed;
the Nene was blanketed from bank to bank.
The sky turned green.
On water, clucking coots dug web-foot spades,
ducking, diving
below a sucking surface closing ranks.

We rowed a furrow through the river,
laden oar blades dredging; ladles
feathering, the sponge-bulk slipped back
dripping with a smack, slap, slop,
slow-motion sinking like a body in a bog
and rising like the emerald undead,
with tiny pops of brothy gas released.
Green quicksand coalesced around the boat.

I trailed a lazy hand.
Sun-simmered sludge, a scoop …
I hurled it at your head.
 "You little minx!" I think that's what you said,
before the world became pea soup.
Knee-deep in laughter,
duck-weed, chuck-weed,
we capsized into each other.

Fish died for lack of oxygen –
but not that afternoon.

Prescription

Warning. This medic may cause
Breathlessness,
Palpitations,
A tingling sensation in the extremities.
Do not exceed the stated dose.

Side effects include
Giddiness,
Euphoria,
Insomnia.
Do not exceed the stated dose.

If you suffer from
Tenderness,
Inflammation of the heart,
Loss of appetite,
Do not exceed the stated dose.

You may experience
Raised blood pressure,
Blurred vision,
Swelling.
Do not exceed the stated dose.

Complete the course
Twice a day, before bedtime.
If you miss your treatment
Seek immediate attention.
Do not exceed the stated dose.

Swallow whole;
Do not bite or crush.
Keep out of the reach and sight of children.
Seduce before the expiry date.
In case of overdose
Change your GP.

Nugget

'This rock contains a diamond,
so I'm told.'
He checks the lump of unassuming ore
up to the light, dense as a fallen meteorite,
South African blue clay, a black hole
flecked with glistering Fools' Gold,
and weighs it in his palm, cupped like a breast;
smoothes it against his thigh as though to bowl
the ball that knocks the bales and wins the Test.

They X-ray oyster shells to check for pearls,
I say. Why not an ultrasound, an MRI,
a scan for differential density?
Let's crack it open, find out, know for sure.

'That nugget is my Koh-I-Noor.
Your grandpa plucked it from the seam
the day he staked his claim at Kimberley.
A talisman. Saved it for luck; gave it to me.
You want to take a hammer to my dream?'

Secret Weapon

When I know I need to send
An urgent email to a friend
But my PC isn't talking to Yahoo …

When tea leaves have blocked the sink
And the kettle's on the blink
And I'm spitting feathers, gasping for a brew …

When I need eight hours or more
But I'm woken up at four
By a cockerel crowing cock-a-doodle-doo …

When I'm struggling with a verse
And my scansion's getting worse
Till my limerick becomes a clerihew …

When I want to curse and cry
'cos the forecast was for 'Dry'
but it's raining and I've planned a barbecue …

When I've flown to Zanzibar
For a fortnight's r&r
But my suitcases have gone to Timbuktu …

When I've put myself in hock
For an antique golden clock
But the dealer says it's only ormolu …

When I say I'd like to play
A new instrument some day
And my kids go out and buy a didgeridoo …

When the *coquilles au gratin*
Need an ounce of parmesan
And the only cheese I have is Port Salut ...

When my underwear is wrong
- bad idea to wear that thong -
and my strapless bra is playing peekaboo ...

When my latest fitness whim
Makes me join the local gym
And I find I've signed up for Advanced Kung Fu ...

When I wake up on the floor
And my back is kinda sore
And I look in the mirror and see that I've got this bloody great dragon tattoo ...

So, when everything I do
Causes yet more ballyhoo
And I've met my Waterloo
Cos my life is plain snafu ...

Then I smile a secret smile and think of you.

Paper City

Paper city. London in my pocket;
Metropolis – reduced, condensed and canned.
This book's a printed oracle – don't knock it.
Street-wise, I hold The Knowledge in my hand.

Its symbols any fool can understand:
The roads are gold, the rivers blue. Rocket-
Science it ain't, but codified, a planned
Paper city: London in my pocket.

Grids quilt the urban sprawl. Block by block it
Presents a labelled, indexed hinterland
With each road named; it's reference run amok;
Metropolis reduced, condensed and canned.

Pick a page at random... Imagine... Stand
At Waterloo. The Eye spins in its socket.
Consult the map to guide me to the Strand.
This book's a printed oracle – don't knock it.

Explorer, pavement pioneer, the Crockett
Of the wild West End, no unknown frontier land
Is closed to me; my route key will unlock it.
Street-wise, I hold the knowledge in my hand.

London – my pocket paper city.

Donation

I hate the very word *phlebotomist*;
I loathe the sight of blood; I'm scared of pain.
I clench and flex my fingers, make a fist.

The thought's enough to make me slit my wrist
Except I lack the nerve to cut a vein.
I hate the very word phlebotomist.

It's not Munchausen's; I'm no masochist,
And yet I volunteer, time and again.
(I clench and flex my fingers, make a fist.)

It's just a little prick, so they insist.
Do needle nurses think I have no brain?
I hate the very word phlebotomist.

I lie and dream of death. The pessimist
Within sees life escaping down their drain.
I clench and flex my fingers, make a fist.

My blood may save a life. Philanthropist
I'm not, but if this helps I won't complain.
Although I hate the word phlebotomist,
I clench and flex my fingers, make a fist.

Bus Stop

You can't get on the bus, guv,
Not with that pot of paint.
Wot if you tripped and knocked the lid off?
We're ill-equipped for getting rid of
Chemicals and toxic spills,
Not to mention cleaning bills.
Speak to Elf 'n' Safety
If you're making a complaint.

You can't get on the bus, mate,
Not with that nasty cough.
Rules are there for your protection.
We don't need no Health Inspection
Swabbing us for cross-infection.
Get a Swine Flu jab injection.
Pass right down the bus, mate,
Use the hand gel and get off.

You can't get on the bus, miss,
Not with an aerosol.
To you it's just a can of hair spray.
That's just what a bomber *would* say.
Take a match, ignite the vapour –
"Boom!" We'd burn like tissue paper.
WMD in cans –
On sale at any mall.

You can't get on the bus, luv,
Not with a noisy child.
ADHD's no excuse for
Letting kids run wild and loose.
Out of pure consideration,
Put him on some medication.
The walk'll calm him down, luv –
Your stop's only one more mile.

You can't get on the bus, Sir,
Not with a rolled umbrella.
Wouldn't do to let the spies in;
That brolly could be tipped with Ricin
To inject a red defector.
Take it up with the Inspector;
Write to your MP, Sir;
Call a cab, there's a good fellah.

You can't get on the bus, man,
Till you're checked by CRB.
Travel safely, unmolested –
Every passenger is tested.
No need to get scared or nervy
Sitting next to someone pervy.
Like it or get on your bike, man.
Rules are rules, so don't blame me.

You can't get on the bus, duck –

Why not? I pose no threat.
I've no poisons, screaming babies,
No knives, no contagious scabies,
High explosives, dogs with rabies;
I don't terrorise old ladies;
I don't wear PJs or Speedos;
I don't fraternise with paedos…
Don't just stand there like a picket –
Do your job and clip my ticket.

Anticipating *The Deathly Hallows*

July reveals the truth: the seventh book
Will bring the Potter series to an end.
When '*Deathly Hallows*' joins the six that lie,
Well-thumbed, upon our shelves, will we have thought
It worth the wait to answer the Big One:
Who wins? Voldemort or Harry with his scar?

Grave questions left unanswered leave a scar
Within our minds. We need this final book
To bring us closure. There is more than one
Plot-line left dangling, leaving a loose end:
Snape murdered Dumbledore without a thought.
Was that a double-bluff, another lie?

No coward, Snape. His loyalties now lie
With the Dark Lord. Or do they? Harry's scar
Gives Voldemort free access to his thought
- a mental link. He won't play by the book
And tell the teachers. No, he thinks he'll end
The war himself, for he's the Chosen One.

More questions ... What's behind the Veil? Which one
Will die off next? And *why* did Albus lie?
Snape's background – was he born at Spinner's End?
Did Lily's sacrifice inflict a scar
On Snape's cold heart? We'll have to read the book.
Is Neville more important than we thought?

Is Snape a vampire? No, perish the thought!
What of the Giants? Is Grawp the only one?
What other spells were in that Potions Book?
Will Pettigrew let sleeping dragons lie?
If Voldemort disappears, will Harry's scar
Go too? Will Ginny win him in the end?

The Horcruxes must meet a sticky end
(assuming Harry finds them). Here's a thought:
Is he, himself, a Horcrux? Does his scar
Entrap a torn soul-fragment? Is he one
Of Voldemort's vessels? Has he lived a lie?
By *his* death will the Dark be brought to book?

So, in the end, who is the Chosen One?
One final thought – Jo Rowling wouldn't lie –
Is 'scar' the last word of the seventh book?

Eating Cheese at Midnight

I ate cheese at bedtime
and hoped I'd dream of you.
I viewed your YouTube clips
until my eyelids drooped,
and hoped I'd dream of you.
I stared at your photo
till your image was etched on my retina,
and hoped I'd dream of you.
I whispered your name into my pillow
and hoped I'd dream of you.
I memorised your midnight Tweet,
switched out the light,
and hoped I'd dream of you.
I tuned my MP3 and drifted off
to the music of your voice,
hoping I'd dream of you.

I dreamed
I was playing Ping-Pong
in a hot air balloon
with a one-eyed, ginger polar bear called Zoe.

Life can be cruel.

Mr Universe

A big kid in a cosmic sweet shop.
Interplanetary pick 'n' mix:
a Galaxy, a Milky Way, a Mars,
a scoop of Popping Plutos, Shooting Stars -
a universe of spectrum-coloured jars.
Iced Rings of Saturn, hot Venusian Rock,
Black Holes, Red Dwarves, a dip of Sherbet Moons,
gob-stopping Hubble bubble-gum Neptunes,
exploding Sun Spots, Sugared Satellites,
bright candied Constellation Clusters,
Melting Meteorites, sharp Acid Asteroids,
dropped in a paper bag and twisted tight
and wrapped in vast infinity, the void.

It's Snowing !

I knew, as soon as those first few
frail flakes blew down and somebody cried, "Snow!"
I *knew* that there were adult things to do
with salt and sand.

But no. I'm standing at the window,
child-eyed, wonder-mouthed and sighing,
"Oooh! Aaah! Oooh!"

I knew I ought to shift my car
before the forecast blizzard struck
and left it stuck out in the street,
marooned in knee-deep drifting dunes.
That would have been the *grown-up* thing to do.
I should have thrown a sheet
to keep the windscreen free,
or taken up a broom to clear
the driveway with my wand in one fell sweep.

I cannot bear to break the spell.
I'm standing at the window
child-eyed, wonder-mouthed and sighing,
"Oooh! Aaah! Oooh!"

I knew, that time I spied
snow shovels on display at B&Q,
that I should buy one for a rainy day…
And if they sold tyre chains at Sainsbury's
I might have bought those too,
or stocked up with a bag of grit.
They say cat litter, new or used, will do
(as long as you remove the shit.)

Instead, my trolley's full
of carrot-nosed fat snowmen,
sledges, snowballs and an Eskimo igloo.
I cannot bear to break the spell.
I'm standing at the window
child-eyed, wonder-mouthed and sighing,
"Oooh! Aaah! Oooh!"

Listening for Sirens

He passed his driving test today;
He's only seventeen
And one month.
Four weeks, fourteen lessons,
Formidable determination –
One might almost say 'driven'.

Now he's borrowed my keys,
Roared off in my Polo,
Solo,
Speeding towards independence.

And I, less useful than I was yesterday,
Am reduced
To running errands now on foot.
Pacing the pavements,
Scanning the traffic
For metallic blue,
Anticipating wreckage,
Listening for sirens.

Perfect Wedding

The local parish church was called St. Rufus in the Wold.
(The tale of bold St. Rufus is a story best untold.)
Since Norman times the church has watched the centuries
    unfold;
it's seen the kind of action that would make your blood run
    cold.

It's witnessed plague and famine, peace and discord, love
    and hate,
survived the Dissolution, Civil War, the rise of State,
seen monarchs reign and fall, ecclesiastical debate,
and now it hosts fund-raisers for the *Lifeboats* and *Relate*.

The liberal-minded vicar of St. Rufus' diocese
 - allegedly - was spotted in the forest hugging trees;
and hums Handel's *Messiah* to his hive of honey bees.
His partner runs the Sunday school and serves divine cream
    teas.

He loves all living creatures. Conservation, he believes,
is holy work. As proof of what the power of prayer achieves,
last harvest time, while men were singing *'Bringing in the
    sheaves',*
a colony of pipistrelles was roosting in the eaves.

The bats slept through the winter, hibernated till the spring,
unseen among the rafters. None suspected anything.
By Easter time the new born broods of young were taking
    wing,
when Barbara set her heart on an idyllic June wedding ...

*

In Top 'n' Tails in all his life the groom had not looked
  smarter.
He waited, nervous, muttering 'Hail Mary, alma mater',
while dreaming of his new wife in her borrowed blue lace
  garter.
She's here! The church re-echoed with the chords of Bach's
  Toccata.

The organist pulled out the stops and played the *Fugue* much
  faster;
the sound shied off the stonework, bounced from column to
  pilaster;
vibration thrilled the air. The windows, walls, the very plaster
shook. That's when the bats woke up and panicked at
  disaster.

A thousand pipistrelles took fright; the church was filled with
  shrieking.
A thousand pipistrelles took flight, though none of them was
  squeaking.
A thousand frenzied flittermouses swooping, swerving,
  wreaking
havoc amongst hats and hair; a congregation freaking,

stampeding, swatting, flapping, batting, ducking, dodging,
  screaming.
The vicar looked on in dismay. He thought he must be
  dreaming.
The bride-to-be dropped to her knees, her wide eyes red and
  streaming,
her perfect day in tatters. All those months of plans and
  scheming!

'You can't harm pipistrelles.' The Rev was deaf to all her
 pleas.
'You're not allowed to smoke them out or move their colonies,
although they may be carriers of rabies or disease.'
The bride paled as she flicked off gritty specs of bat faeces.

'Do you ...?' 'I do.' She begged the organist to please refrain
from playing out *'Here Comes the Bride'* and spooking bats
 again.
Her smile was hardly joyful, more a rictus of disdain
as down the aisle she marched while sweeping bat shit with
 her train.

The vicar shook the hand of each dishevelled wedding guest,
astonished that a cloud of bats could leave them so
 distressed.
Apologising for the mess, he made a last request,
'Tread carefully in the graveyard. Don't disturb the adder's
 nest.'

Quick Brown Fox

I'm quick, I'm brown, I'm foxy ... Watch me jump,
break covert, run and vanish in thin air,
then double back, hide in the rotten stump.
That mangy mongrel didn't have a prayer ...

I jink, twist, weave and zigzag like a hare,
or go to earth and rest beneath a clump
of grass, downwind. Hounds, catch me if you dare!
I'm quick, I'm brown, I'm foxy. Watch me jump!

The hunt will claim my brush and pads and dump
my body for the drooling dogs to share.
I'll wait, then, when the pack has crossed the sump,
break covert, run and vanish in thin air.

Too crafty, wily, sly for any snare,
I'll drown my musky scent under the pump
- their view-halloo won't drive me to despair –
then double back, hide in the rotten stump.

I had a near escape – some canine chump
once had me cornered; gave me quite a scare.
I leapt over his head, the lazy lump!
That mangy mongrel didn't have a prayer.

I'd rather be with vixen in my lair,
not fleeing from the thudding, thundering thump
of hooves; nor being baited like a bear.
Beware! I'm not yet grizzled, grey and plump –
I'm quick, I'm brown, I'm foxy ...

The Icing on the Cake

I'm going to roll
this Christmas up
into a ball
of marzipan –
baubles, lights,
last minute shopping,
turkey, pies,
non-dropping trees.
Goodwill to all.
And then, perhaps, I'll mould
a sweet, thin, yellow man
from almond paste
so's not to waste the scraps.
My Christmas voodoo doll.
I'm sticking holly in
instead of pins.

For Geoffrey   *For G B*

You chewed up Chaucer
with the vigour we reserved for gum,
extruding warped vowels on your tongue
and blowing huge, wet, wobbly pearls of verse
into the class. They shimmered in the gawping air
above our heads
and burst against indifference.
We squirmed on your behalf.
For all we cared it might have been old Norse,
or Klingon, Esperanto, ancient Greek.
It was all *geek* to us.
We sniggered then, as only schoolgirls can.

Your shabby corduroy suit hung loose
as though your mum had bought it years ago
and left you room to grow.
All angles – elbows, chin (but poet's hands) –
you had the seedy, undernourished look
of someone germinated in the dark,
cooped-up indoors with curtains closed,
a weedy, pale, scoop-shouldered Romeo.
Intelligence and zeal earned zero marks:
by *Jackie* quiz criteria, your score was low.

It took some nerve to stand there, brutally
exposed to our coy, cruel scrutiny
and persevere. Your duty: to impart
a taste for literature and art
to blinkered teens who didn't give a tinker's cuss,
who sat counting not syllables
but minutes till the bell and then the bus.
Dear Geoffrey, you were so wasted on us.

Floreat Verbum

Keep your carnations and bin the bouquet;
Stuff your chrysanthemums. Chuck 'em away.
Talk to me if you've got something to say.
   Tell me you love me; don't say it with flowers.

Lilies for sympathy; roses for guilt;
Orchids – a quick fix when tears have been spilt...
Thanks a bunch, buddy – but *words* wouldn't wilt.
   Tell me you love me; don't say it with flowers.

They say words are cheap – it depends what you're saying.
You can't buy me love – that depends how you're paying.
No gift of the gab? Then you'd better start praying...
   Tell me you love me; don't say it with flowers.

Pay me a compliment. Please, keep it verbal.
Cough up the charm like a cat with a fur ball.
Flattery's oral, not floral or herbal.
   Tell me you love me; don't say it with flowers.

Don't try to get round me with champagne and chocs -
The secret can stay in its Black Magic box.
For one magic *word*... Opportunity knocks!
   Tell me you love me; don't say it with flowers.

Actions speak louder... (Or that's what they teach).
Read my lips, petal. Practise what I preach:
Save the grand gestures and give me a speech.
   Tell me you love me; don't say it with flowers.

Are you too tongue-tied to say what you feel?
Bugger the language of flowers. Here's the deal:
Forget Interflora – just give me the spiel.
   Tell *me you love me; don't say it with flowers.*

Intensive Care

I sat out the Spring
in the pink chintz gloom
of that blinds drawn
relatives' waiting room,
anaesthetised
by disbelief;
rehearsing my grief.

Some days we shared our space
with newly stricken faces,
twisting tissues, failing gamely not to weep
in front of strangers.
As if we cared.
They rarely stayed
more than a week.

I've memorised the notice-board by heart,
the tactful, star-burst practical advice:
flowers, showers, drinking water,
canteen times, the Patients' Charter,
multi-cultural translator,
chaplaincy, no smoking, car park fees.
Suggestions please…
I've ticked the box
agreeing that a fish tank would be nice.

Sawdust picnics on our knees:
plastic rolls, stewed tepid teas
(we dare not ask the nurse to fill our flask).

Brave the intercom and pass
into that timeless, twilight zone:
a shrine to high technology
and dedicated medics working

miracles
with *Hibiscrub* and hope.

Operation.
Complication.
Intubation.
Ventilation.
Medication.
Sedation.
Sedation.

Input, output,
calibration,
pulse-rate, heart-rate, respiration,
cell count, swab analyses,
progress measured by degrees,
test results,
examinations,
points, percentage calculation.
solve the physical equation.

How can the staff
appreciate her worth?
So much more
than a score on a graph;
greater by far than the sum
of her charts.
This is my Mum.

For Barbara

Barbara Leach, 1959-1979

Our parents warned us not to walk alone,
But, sassy, young, defiant, we knew best.
Had we but known, Barbara; had we but known.

He watched you leave the pub and set off home.
Was it your smile, your style, the way you dressed?
Your parents warned you not to walk alone …

Dark alleyway: a hammer shattered bone;
Eight times the spiked screw-driver stabbed your chest.
Had you but known, Barbara; had you but known.

No time to scream for help or find your phone …
Because of men like Sutcliffe, Wright and West
Our parents warned us not to walk alone.

He dumped you, wrapped in carpet, topped with stone -
He thought you were a hooker, like the rest.
Had he but known, Barbara; had he but known.

At school we felt the whole world was our own;
Our futures stretched before us, boundless, blessed;
Our parents warned us not to walk alone.
Had we but known, Barbara; had we but known.

The Smell of Wet Cats

The rain has spoiled their game.
Fine toys so tantalising with their buzz,
their scurry, hover, flutter, slither, hop,
have slunk to shelter:
burrows dry beyond the swipe of paws;
tall boughs too inaccessible
for even kitten intrepidity,
where sullen, silent, bouffant sparrows hunch
like secretaries nursing lunchtime perms
in overhanging doorways, waiting
for that big break in the clouds.

Porcupine-spined, they lick and fret.
Four amber eyes impale me with reproach.
Failed weather god,
I'm burying my face in spiky fur,
inhaling mystery and musk,
an earthen, elemental, wet cat smell.

Mothering Sunday

Eighty-four and chippy as a meerkat,
Mum's wearing jeans,
a sweatshirt, Wellingtons and straw sunhat
- she's dressed for gardening, for planting beans.
She takes my hot-house bunch and trims the stalks,
recalls her sister's wedding, how the scent
of freesia filled the tiny church; enshrines
the vase upon the mantel as she talks:
hand-picked fresh memories, fragrant still, intense
as only yesterday, pressed in her mind;

declines Plan A (a scenic drive, then lunch);
suggests Plan B:
a spot of gardening. I have a hunch
she has a list of jobs lined up for me.
I'm not wrong there. First task: clean out the pond.
It's silted up with slime and rotten leaves.
*"Just catch the fish and stick them in that tub.
Here, use this net."* I feel like I've been conned.
She brings me buckets, gloves; I roll my sleeves.
"The butyl liner needs a thorough scrub."

Two siphons spurt a fertilising slick
of sludge black gold,
till, clogged, they sputter, falter, fail. The trick
is not to suck the hose, so I've been told,
but synchronise the letting go, the plunge
into the depths. Mum's on the lower lawn,
thumb capped upon the pipe, waiting my call.
It brims. *"One, two, three ... Go!"* I shout. Even gunge
will rush to fill a vacuum. Don't scorn
the laws of physics, gravitational fall.

Knee-deep in foetid, smooth organic ooze,
gas bubbles popping
on the surface like fermenting booze,
I'm dredging bucketfuls of noxious slop.
The lily pad's an iceberg of a plant:
beneath the water level, massive roots
extend to Australasia. We hoist
it out and hack it into clumps I can't
quite lift. Wet goo is squelching in my boots;
my trouser legs are clingy, clammy, moist ...

We stand back and survey our handiwork.
The pool refills.
Sleek goldfish dart and weave, going berserk
to feel the cool, clear water in their gills.
Pond maintenance! What better way to say
'I love you, Mum', to grant her quirky wish?
We both look like we've just escaped noyade
instead of celebrating Mother's Day.

You cannot put a price on happy fish.
Some things cannot be written on a card.

Forgotten

Ignored, I'm seething, plotting, hurling spears
of fury, boiling vitriol, a storm
of imprecation. All he hears

are honeyed words as I invoke a swarm
of killer bees. Revenge, where is thy sting?
This slip will cost him chocolate, champagne,

some rocks – and here I'm talking total bling.
How can I shake that ego-plated, vain
complacency? What vengeance can I wreak?

Emotional amnesia is an Art:
he's annually perfecting his technique;
I'm looking daggers, aiming for his heart.

Rachel

Rachel Corrie, 1979 - 2003

"Rachel who? Sorry."
"Rachel Corrie."
"Oh, wasn't she that Yank, that peacenik girl, that crank,
run over by a tank?"
   By a bulldozer, actually. In Gaza.

Her death, in Palestine,
outraged the news for two indignant days
before the headlines were invaded
by Baghdad.
Front pages fed
on bigger bloodshed.

Three years later, her life
plays on stage.
For an hour or more
the West End is transformed into Rafah,
the theatre of war.

'My Name is Rachel Corrie'.
No longer anonymous –
what title could be more eponymous?
Ovations, applause, awards and acclaim –
posthumous fame.
A script that rips complacency to shame,
paints her as neither sinner nor a saint.

Was it naïve to believe
in passive resistance?
To think that the massive Israeli machine
might be brought to the brink,
that the fighting would yield
to the force of that white human shield?

Two thousand years ago
another doomed idealist
would have thought her right.

She never sought martyrdom,
unlike the bombers of today
– the countrymen for whom she died –
whose suicides
with *Semtex* on their backs,
betray her sacrifice.
At least she tried.

Her diaries reveal
a person of unfashionable zeal,
and fiery, feisty, passionate desire
to make a difference;
raw energy – the sort that fuels revolt
and, sometimes, brings it to a halt;
a girl who felt man's cruellest fault was apathy.
She left her home and friends to lend relief
to strangers in a foreign land;
to stand and die for her belief.

And I (who've never marched for any cause,
nor broken any laws,
nor spoken out in protest, called for peace,
have never been arrested by police,
nor freed lab animals to pull a stunt,
nor sabotaged a hunt,
have never joined a picket line,
picked up a ticket or a speeding fine)
– politics aside –
I'm humbled by her zest, her drive,
her courage in the face of life and death,
by her capacity to care.

Coming home on the train, I cried
for the waste of two lives
– hers and mine.

Slide Viewer

The slides are stacked like bullion in a case,
Card-mounted ingots, golden memories,
Packed, labelled, numbered (year, date, time and place);
Snaps, *Kodakcolour* shot ephemeries.
Dark squares, frame frozen, capture shadow ghosts
Of holidays, trapped in transparent night.
We post them in the viewer slot like toast;
Press down to bring our yesterdays to light.
My father, paddling, holds me by the hand.
His features scowl annoyance, knotted, hint
At disapproval. Now I understand
The narrowed eyes, the dazzled frown, the squint.
The realisation slices like a knife:
I've had the sun behind me all my life.

Alone

Grief landmines time.
Each hour I lose a limb.
A single sniper trains his sights
upon my heart;
each bullet bears my name –
an unused cup,
a pair of Christmas trousers never worn,
a magazine of loaded memories.

Grief lies in ambush
in an empty fireside chair,
a threadbare phrase that fells me unawares,
the trailer for the rugby on TV,
chrysanthemums unwatered in their pots,
the night time ritual with lock and key
- a fusillade of private parting shots.

Grief strings its tripwires
through the silent house: a hat, a coat,
a dry toothbrush; an unsigned card
he bought but never wrote.

Unarmed, I soldier on.
Each day a battle in a lonely war.

www.ingramcontent.com/pod-product-compliance
Lightning Source LLC
Chambersburg PA
CBHW071332040426
42444CB00009B/2135